THE SNOW DEAD

Marc Zegans

Červená Barva Press
Somerville, Massachusetts

Červená Barva Press
P.O. Box 440357
W. Somerville, MA 02144-3222

www.cervenabarvapress.com

Bookstore: www.thelostbookshelf.com

Cover art: "Oil painting by Alexander Schaepkens of a
view of Maastricht, the Netherlands."

Cover Design: William J. Kelle

ISBN: 978-1-950063-39-0

THE SNOW DEAD

They leave their offerings

Quit
  Falls.

I was surprised by the gravel
Scattered like crumble
On top of the glacier.

I had imagined it slick, glassy
At the surface, not gritted
And yet, this shrinking
Cracked MASSIF held tread.

I leaped across the crevasses
In the sun-cold, un-bleaked
Afternoon light, turning back
To look into the deeper cuts
Bluing in the narrows.

We peer into history, as we stare
Below the root line. Looking up
Is more complex, a tracing of past
And a hurtling expansion
But in the ice all is dead, purified
Crystalline, and yet blue like life.

The offerings are left on the surface
Testamentary evidence of the killing.
The bodies in ice were never offered
Merely preserved, accidents in waiting.
On the surface, there is no recovery.
The snow dead decay more slowly
The flies do not swarm. We watch.

At distance, they appear as black marks
The work of a spare calligrapher
Who enlivens the field by its small rupture.
Gradient enters as we approach
First tone, then hue, then texture
Finally wetness. We see the slicked blood
The glistening hair by the wound.
The seeping of fluids draws raptors.

A fox lies on fresh snow.
Its neck broke, slight steam
Exiting its once clever mouth.

Before I knew how to make snow angels
There was the corpse on the bowed lawn
Arms thrown wide, palms up, fingers spread
Shoed toes pointed toward the sidewalk.

When the first snow came
The uncut grass poked up
Leaving small circles
Around stiffened stems
Taking season as aberration.

"The souls speak louder
In the graveyard
Under winter snow"
She said, leaving
Footprints amongst
The headstones.

I can't tell you anything.
I missed the opportunity.
My bones tell no tales.
The snow heaves over
My recent-filled grave.
In spring it will sink
Bedded, then, with sod.

We take the frozen rictus
As a grin, as if there was
A secret, zygomatic joke
Less than cosmic, merely
Private, as if, in the life
Cut short at the moment
Of death, wry truth is given.
It is a lie we tell ourselves.

She was a pin-up model [1]
In World War II, known
To millions in glossies
Then forgotten, neglected
Living still into her 80s
Alone in a weathered house
Above Route 2, attic filled
With curling stills, dried ink
And bushels of love letters

The smell of dark wool tweed
Over dark wool suits
Black shoes not meant for snow
Leather gloves that will pinch
And stain when touched by salt.

I would walk through the woods
Scavenging fallen branches,
The leaf stripped deadwood,
Cut it, stack it and leave it to dry.
I could tell by feel how long it
Had rested in the snow, and why.

"Don't be fooled," he said
"Many of the snow dead
Have life in them yet.
Some are simply resting
Others hiding in winter
Most don't know
Warmth a memory lost."

Streetlights and silence in this cold
Place lit by candles, convenience store
Chocolate donuts and well-aged wine
Our only food, as we sit on the floor
Staring out at the snow-cleaned street.
It's four AM. We are the only two people
Alive. You have no power, nor I
But there is electricity between us.

There was always the kid
Who left in winter, after
A beating, pissed pants
Yellowing the snow
Never heard from
Hardly remembered
Family erased
As the house was bought
And made fresh in spring.

You have collapsed all my angels
All the times I fell back and flapped
My arms at 6 AM in the newly fallen
As if in the flurry, I could leave a mark.
Before I could rise, you were stomping
Free all evidence of my angel's visit
Killing his whisper-trace in the fragile snow.

They carried the body out of the woods.
An unseen fall off a granite ledge.
The cold a kindness, bringing sleep
A quiet ride into the hereafter.
There was no sign of panic or fear
Not even pain, as he lay there unable.
There was no sign of who he was.
An identity would be given—but that is no sign.

We feel the stillness
Witness the white
Are quieted
The death is a mark
In the snow – a stroke
In the larger picture
In spring, it is central
A tear in the fabric, there
A loss—now, a return

ABOUT THE AUTHOR

Marc Zegans is a poet and creative development advisor. He is the author of five previous collections of poems, *The Underwater Typewriter*, *Boys in the Woods*, *Pillow Talk*, *The Book of Clouds*, and *La Commedia Sotterranea: Swizzle Felt's First Folio form the Typewriter Underground*; two spoken word albums *Night Work*, and *Marker and Parker*, and the immersive theatrical productions *Mum and Shaw*, and *The Typewriter Underground*. *The Snow Dead* debuted theatrically in Erotic Eclectic's "Sin-aesthetic" at the Lost Church during San Francisco's 2019 Lit Crawl. Marc lives by the coast in Northern California. His poetry can be found at marczegans.com, and he can be reached for creative advisory services at mycreativedevelopment.com.

CPSIA information can be obtained
at www.ICGtesting.com
Printed in the USA
LVHW110840030520
654646LV00007B/491